W9-BGT-545

Elegy

PITT POETRY SERIES

Ed Ochester, *Editor*

Elegy

Larry Levis

Edited with a foreword by Philip Levine

UNIVERSITY OF PITTSBURGH PRESS

Published by the University of Pittsburgh Press,
Pittsburgh, Pa.15261

Manufactured in the United States of America
Printed on acid-free paper
10 9 8 7 6 5 4 3 2 1

Library of Congress Cataloging-in-Publication data and acknowledgments
are located at the end of this book.

A CIP catalog record for this book is available from
the British Library.

THE PUBLICATION OF THIS
BOOK IS SUPPORTED BY A GRANT
FROM THE
PENNSYLVANIA COUNCIL ON THE ARTS

Contents

Foreword

PHILIP LEVINE

W hat follows is a collection of poems, a unified book I hope, carved from the work Larry Levis left behind when he died suddenly and unexpectedly in May 1996. Larry and I had spoken on the phone only a few days before he died; he planned then to bring an "all-but-completed manuscript" with him when he returned to California in June to visit his mother in the Central Valley. That visit, of course, never took place, nor did the meeting of the two of us during which we'd planned to look over this new book, portions of which I'd already received in the mail during the past few years. I truly have no way of knowing what that "all-but-completed manuscript" would have looked like, for what was finally placed in my hands were a great many poems in various drafts and stages of completion all written since the completion of his collection *The Widening Spell of the Leaves* (1991).

I have written elsewhere of my long relationship with Larry. I met him when he was a freshman at California State University, Fresno. He was the most gifted and determined young poet I have ever had the good fortune to have in one of my classes. We soon became friends, and for over twenty-five years we had exchanged poems and drafts of poems. For at least fifteen years he had become my essential critic. I do not know if I filled that role in his poetic life. My educated guess is that I filled that role until about 1990; somewhere around that time he became his own essential critic. Before his death I had seen only a fragment—probably one out of four—of the poems in the present collection. Nonetheless, his sister, Sheila Brady, the person I believe he was closest to, asked me to edit this book, and I accepted the task.

I have rewritten nothing. I have revised nothing. I have done my best to determine which poems Larry felt were completed or had gone as far as he could take them. I've tried to include the final or the last versions of these poems. By no means have I included all the poems I believed Larry considered finished. I had no choice but to trust my own taste; I believe that if we had had that June meeting I would have helped him eliminate those poems not up to his own very high standards. He had helped me shape my last three books and had advised me to eliminate a number of poems. I had done the same for him with all his previous volumes.

I could say that this time I was on my own, but it would not be true, for two of Larry's oldest friends, superb poets in their own right, were invaluable; without their advice I truly doubt that this collection would exist. Peter Everwine first showed me that Larry was not cannibalizing certain passages from some poems in order to heighten and enlarge other more ambitious poems, but that in fact he was using these motifs or "riffs" to unify the collection he had in mind. Peter's taste seemed unerring, and I used it almost without fail in determining what belonged in the collection and what did not. To David St. John I owe the scheme which finally determined the structure of the book. His sense of the shape the collection required was far more judicious and compelling than my own, and so I adopted it with some modifications. Without the generous guidance of these two poets I would still be at sea and this collection would not exist. All the final determinations were my own, and if there are mistakes in taste and judgment here they are mine. Greg Donovan, Mary Flinn, and Amy Tudor, Larry's three close and loyal friends in Richmond, his final home, worked tirelessly to supply me with (and when it was possible to date) the various versions of the poems, the ones that are here and the ones that are not. Without their help there would be no book.

The poems themselves require no introduction from me or anyone. They were written by one of our essential poets at the very height of his powers. His early death is a staggering loss for our poetry, but what he left is a major achievement that will enrich our lives for as long as poetry matters.

I

The Two Trees

My name in Latin is light to carry & victorious.
I'd read late in the library, then
Walk out past the stacks, rows, aisles

Of books, where the memoirs of battles slowly gave way
To case histories of molestation & abuse.

The black windows looked out onto the black lawn.

❧

Friends, in the middle of this life, I was embraced
By failure. It clung to me & did not let go.
When I ran, brother limitation raced

Beside me like a shadow. Have you never
Felt like this, everyone you know,

Turning, the more they talked, into . . .

Acquaintances? So many strong opinions!

And when I tried to speak—
Someone always interrupting. My head ached.
And I would walk home in the blackness of winter.

I still had two friends, but they were trees.
One was a box elder, the other a horse chestnut.

I used to stop on my way home & talk to each

Of them. The three of us lived in Utah then, though
We never learned why, me, *acer negundo*, & the other
One, whose name I can never remember.

"Everything I have done has come to nothing.
It is not even worth mocking," I would tell them,
And then I would look up into their limbs & see

How they were covered in ice. "You do not even
Have a car any*more*," one of them would answer.

All their limbs glistening above me,
No light was as cold or clear.

I got over it, but I was never the same,

Hearing the snow change to rain & the wind swirl,
And the gull's cry, that it could not fly out of.

In time, in a few months, I could walk beneath
Both trees without bothering to look up
Anymore, neither at the one

Whose leaves & trunk were being slowly colonized by
Birds again, nor at the other, sleepier, more slender

One, that seemed frail, but was really

Oblivious to everything. Simply oblivious to it,
With the pale leaves climbing one side of it,
An obscure sheen in them,

And the other side, for some reason, black, bare,
The same, almost irresistible, carved indifference

In the shape of its limbs

As if someone's cries for help
Had been muffled by them once, concealed there,

Her white flesh just underneath the slowly peeling bark

—while the joggers swerved around me & I stared—

Still tempting me to step in, find her,

And possess her completely.

In 1967

Some called it the Summer of Love; & although the clustered,
Motionless leaves that overhung the streets looked the same
As ever, the same as they did every summer, in 1967,
Anybody with three dollars could have a vision.
And who wouldn't want to know what it felt like to be
A cedar waxwing landing with a flutter of gray wings
In a spruce tree, & then disappearing into it,
For only three dollars? And now I know; its flight is ecstasy.
No matter how I look at it, I also now know that
The short life of a cedar waxwing is more pure pleasure
Than anyone alive can still be sane, & bear.
And remember, a cedar waxwing doesn't mean a thing,
Qua cedar or *qua* waxwing, nor could it have earned
That kind of pleasure by working to become a better
Cedar waxwing. They're all the same.
Show me a bad cedar waxwing, for example, & I mean
A really morally corrupted cedar waxwing, & you'll commend
The cage they have reserved for you, resembling heaven.

Some people spent their lives then, having visions.
But in my case, the morning after I dropped mescaline
I had to spray Johnson grass in a vineyard of Thompson Seedless
My father owned—& so, still feeling the holiness of all things
Living, holding the spray gun in one hand & driving with the other,
The tractor pulling the spray rig & its sputtering motor—
Row after row, I sprayed each weed I found
That looked enough like Johnson grass, a thing alive that's good
For nothing at all, with a mixture of malathion & diesel fuel,
And said to each tall weed, as I coated it with a lethal mist,
Dominus vobiscum, &, sometimes, *mea culpa*, until
It seemed boring to apologize to weeds, & insincere as well.
For in a day or so, no more than that, the weeds would turn
Disgusting hues of yellowish orange & wither away. I still felt
The bird's flight in my body when I thought about it, the wing ache,
Lifting heaven, locating itself somewhere just above my slumped
Shoulders, & part of me taking wing. I'd feel it at odd moments
After that on those long days I spent shoveling vines, driving trucks
And tractors, helping swamp fruit out of one orchard
Or another, but as the summer went on, I felt it less & less.

As the summer went on, some were drafted, some enlisted
In a generation that would not stop falling, a generation
Of leaves sticking to body bags, & when they turned them
Over, they floated back to us on television, even then,
In the Summer of Love, in 1967,
When riot police waited beyond the doors of perception,
And the best thing one could do was get arrested.

The Oldest Living Thing in L.A.

At Wilshire & Santa Monica I saw an opossum
Trying to cross the street. It was late, the street
Was brightly lit, the opossum would take
A few steps forward, then back away from the breath
Of moving traffic. People coming out of the bars
Would approach, as if to help it somehow.
It would lift its black lips & show them
The reddened gums, the long rows of incisors,
Teeth that went all the way back beyond
The flames of Troy & Carthage, beyond sheep
Grazing rock-strewn hills, fragments of ruins
In the grass at San Vitale. It would back away
Delicately & smoothly, stepping carefully
As it always had. It could mangle someone's hand
In twenty seconds. Mangle it for good. It could
Sever it completely from the wrist in forty.
There was nothing to be done for it. Someone
Or other probably called the LAPD, who then
Called Animal Control, who woke a driver, who
Then dressed in mailed gloves, the kind of thing
Small knights once wore into battle, who gathered
Together his pole with a noose on the end,
A light steel net to snare it with, someone who hoped
The thing would have vanished by the time he got there.

Anastasia & Sandman

The brow of a horse in that moment when
The horse is drinking water so deeply from a trough
It seems to inhale the water, is holy.

I refuse to explain.

When the horse had gone the water in the trough,
All through the empty summer,

Went on reflecting clouds & stars.

The horse cropping grass in a field,
And the fly buzzing around its eyes, are more real
Than the mist in one corner of the field.

Or the angel hidden in the mist, for that matter.

Members of the Committee on the Ineffable,
Let me illustrate this with a story, & ask you all
To rest your heads on the table, cushioned,
If you wish, in your hands, &, if you want,
Comforted by a small carton of milk
To drink from, as you once did, long ago,
When there was only a curriculum of beach grass,
When the University of Flies was only a distant humming.

In Romania, after the war, Stalin confiscated
The horses that had been used to work the fields.
"You won't need horses now," Stalin said, cupping
His hand to his ear, "Can't you hear the tractors
Coming in the distance? I hear them already."

The crowd in the Callea Victoria listened closely
But no one heard anything. In the distance
There was only the faint glow of a few clouds.
And the horses were led into boxcars & emerged
As the dimly remembered meals of flesh
That fed the starving Poles
During that famine, & part of the next one—
In which even words grew thin & transparent,

Like the pale wings of ants that flew
Out of the oldest houses, & slowly
What had been real in words began to be replaced
By what was not real, by the not exactly real.
"Well, not exactly, but . . ." became the preferred
Administrative phrasing so that the man
Standing with his hat in his hands would not guess
That the phrasing of a few words had already swept
The earth from beneath his feet. "That horse I had,
He was more real than any angel,
The housefly, when I had a house, was real too,"
Is what the man thought.
Yet it wasn't more than a few months
Before the man began to wonder, talking
To himself out loud before the others,
"Was the horse real? Was the house real?"
An angel flew in and out of the high window
In the factory where the man worked, his hands
Numb with cold. He hated the window & the light
Entering the window & he hated the angel.
Because the angel could not be carved into meat
Or dumped into the ossuary & become part
Of the landfill at the edge of town,
It therefore could not acquire a soul,
And resembled in significance nothing more
Than a light summer dress when the body has gone.

The man survived because, after a while,
He shut up about it.

Stalin had a deep understanding of the *kulaks*,
Their sense of marginalization & belief in the land;

That is why he killed them all.

Members of the Committee on Solitude, consider
Our own impoverishment & the progress of that famine,
In which, now, it is becoming impossible
To feel anything when we contemplate the burial,
Alive, in a two-hour period, of hundreds of people.

Who were not clichés, who did not know they would be
The illegible blank of the past that lives in each
Of us, even in some guy watering his lawn

On a summer night. Consider

The death of Stalin & the slow, uninterrupted
Evolution of the horse, a species no one,
Not even Stalin, could extinguish, almost as if
What could not be altered was something
Noble in the look of its face, something

Incapable of treachery.

Then imagine, in your planning proposals,
The exact moment in the future when an angel
Might alight & crawl like a fly into the ear of a horse,
And then, eventually, into the brain of a horse,
And imagine further that the angel in the brain
Of this horse is, for the horse cropping grass
In the field, largely irrelevant, a mist in the corner
Of the field, something that disappears,
The horse thinks, when weight is passed through it,
Something that will not even carry the weight
Of its own father
On its back, the horse decides, & so demonstrates
This by swishing at a fly with its tail, by continuing
To graze as the dusk comes on & almost until it is night.

Old contrivers, daydreamers, walking chemistry sets,
Exhausted chimneysweeps of the spaces
Between words, where the Holy Ghost tastes just
Like the dust it is made of,
Let's tear up our lecture notes & throw them out
The window.
Let's do it right now before wisdom descends upon us
Like a spiderweb over a burned-out theater marquee,
Because what's the use?
I keep going to meetings where no one's there,
And contributing to the discussion;

And besides, behind the angel hissing in its mist
Is a gate that leads only into another field,
Another outcropping of stones & withered grass, where
A horse named Sandman & a horse named Anastasia
Used to stand at the fence & watch the traffic pass.
Where there were outdoor concerts once, in summer,
Under the missing & innumerable stars.

Photograph: Migrant Worker, Parlier, California, 1967

I'm going to put Johnny Dominguez right here
In front of you on this page so that
You won't mistake him for something else,
An idea, for example, of how oppressed
He was, rising with his pan of Thompson Seedless
Grapes from a row of vines. The band
On his white straw hat darkened by sweat, is,
He would remind you, just a hatband.
His hatband. He would remind you of that.
As for the other use, this unforeseen
Labor you have subjected him to, the little
Snacks & white wine of the opening he must
Bear witness to, he would remind you
That he was not put on this earth
To be an example of something else,
Johnny Dominguez, he would hasten to
Remind you, in his chaste way of saying things,
Is not to be used as an example of anything
At all, not even, he would add after
A second or so, that greatest of all
Impossibilities, that unfinishable agenda
Of the stars, that fact, Johnny Dominguez.

Shiloh

When my friends found me after I'd been blown
Into the limbs of a tree, my arms were wide open.
It must have looked as if I were welcoming something,

Awakening to it. They left my arms like that,
Not because of the triumphant, mocking shape they took
In death, & not because the withheld breath

Of death surprised my arms, made them believe,
For a split second, that they were really wings
Instead of arms, & had always been wings. No, it was

Because, by the time the others found me, I had been
Sitting there for hours with my arms spread wide,
And when they tried, they couldn't bend them back,

Couldn't cross them over my chest as was the custom,
So that the corpses that kept lining the tracks
Might look like sleeping choir boys. They were

No choir, although in death they were restored
To all they had been once. They were just boys
Fading back into the woods & the ravines again.

I could see that much in the stingy, alternating light
And shade the train threw out as it began to slow,
And the rest of us gazed out from what seemed to me

One endless, empty window on what had to be.
What had to be came nearer in a sudden hiss of brakes,
The glass clouding with our reflections as we stood.

Arms & wings. They'll mock you one way or the other.

The Poem Returning as an Invisible Wren to the World

Once, there was a poem. No one read it & the poem
Grew wise. It grew wise & then it grew thin,
No one could see it perched on the woman's
Small shoulders as she went on working beside

The gray conveyer belt with the others.
No one saw the poem take the shape of a wren,
A wren you could look through like a window,
And see all the bitterness of the world

In the long line of shoulders & faces bending
Over the gleaming, machined parts that passed
Before them, the faces transformed by the grace
And ferocity of a wren, a wren you could look

Through, like a lens, to see them working there.
This is not about how she threw herself into the river,
For she didn't, nor is it about the way her breasts
Looked in moonlight, nor about moonlight at all.

This is about the surviving curve of the bridge
Where she listened to the river whispering to her,
When the wren flew off & left her there,
With the knowledge of it singing in her blood.

By which the wind avenges. By which the rain avenges.
By which even the limb of a dead tree leaning
Above the white, swirling mouth of an eddy
In the river that once ran beside the factory window

Where she once worked, shall be remembered
When the dead come back, & take their places
Beside her on the line, & the gray conveyor belt
Starts up with its raspy hum again. Like a heaven's.

II

The Thief in the Painting

Thirsty all through Lent, thirsty on feast days too,
I was meant to be part of the picture,
Born to be the thief with his face averted,

Only a stone's throw from the crowd,
An exiled white gleam of flesh in the background
Before the bare hill blurs into pines,

And the pines into . . . ? So it is written.
After the crowds went off to their amusements
And the three of us were left to wither away,

I kept meaning to ask, then kept forgetting to—
Staring off, and gliding out of my flesh on my stare—
Forgetting what and who it was I had wanted to ask.

I remember now a gust of wind on the dry hill
In that moment, and the sore screech of a wheel,
An endless screeching, off in the distance somewhere,

And the wind carving an idle shape in the dust.
In that moment when you pause after a long day
Of scheming and calculation, the moment just before

The wine is poured at your table, the afternoon light
Quivering a little on the bleached fronds of the palms
Above the Piazza dei Poppolo, the moment when Craxi

Emerges dripping with sweat from the Senate, think
Of me, so necessary for the balance of the composition,
So necessary to the street that goes on being a street,

That never once rises up into the fine spun dust of heaven,
As you watch it quickening with life and will watch it . . .
How many more times? Twenty? Fifty? Think of me,

For who among you now could say with certainty
Which thief I was, could tell which mark blurred
By rain in a ledger once meant me, which meant

That linen on a stick who was once my friend,
And which meant the possessed boy who went on speaking
To shapes he saw before him in the air, shapes

Which I knew, even as I turned my face away from him
Then, out of a serene contempt, were nothing more,
Could never be anything more, than what was really there—

The hard, pure, furiously indifferent faces of thieves.

Boy in Video Arcade

Some see a lake of fire at the end of it,
Or heaven's guesswork, something always to be sketched in.

I see a sullen boy in a video arcade.
He's the only one there at this hour, shoulders slightly bent above a machine.
I see the pimples on his chin, the scuffed linoleum on the floor.

I like the close-up, the detail. I like the pointlessness of it,
And the way it hasn't imagined an ending to all this yet,

The boy never bothering to look up as the sun comes out
In the late morning, because, Big Deal, the mist evaporating & rising.

So Death blows his little fucking trumpet, Big Deal, says the boy.

I don't see anything at the end of it except an endlessness,

The beauty parlors, the palm reader's unlighted sign, the mulberry trees
Fading out before the billboard of the chiropractor.

The lake of fire's just an oil speck.
I don't see anything at the end of it, & I suppose that is what is wrong with me,

Among the other things. And it's slow work, because of all the gauzy light,

It's hard to pick out anything.

The Cook Grew Lost in His Village, the Village in the Endless Shuffling of Their Cards

One by one the gods grew wearier of their games,
Of the world that came & went in the chipped paint of its toys;
At last only two of them were left, sitting outside the café.
The backs of their cards, as they multiplied
On the mildewing tablecloth,
Displayed nude women in the finite poses of desire. Some live,
Some don't, the cards said. So the girl with a bad cough
Who won't last out the month brings up
A little more blood each dawn, while the boy who saw
The world turn into a thin husk of lies, & who longed
To be cold seed on the wind, must live on at the end of the Emperor's
Leash, for as long as the Emperor sleeps.

Aweem Away, Aweem Away, sings the little radio
On the kitchen windowsill. But the cook isn't listening.
He knows all feasts are delusions, that the scent of immortality
And the savor of oblivion are one, that both give off
A whiff of something rancid like the egg in a workman's lunchpail
Discovered at the muddy edges of a pond.
The two of them at their table go on playing cards & laughing,
A bleached kite in some telephone lines above them, the sky
Above that. Some live, some don't. The cook thinks
That the blood the girl coughs up at dawn
Onto her pillow would be enough reality for anyone, if anyone
Else had seen it, as he did, for the blood is
Her spreading out onto the pillow without anyone asking
The girl's opinion about it, & the laughter issuing out of these two
Bent over their cards enters the thought of the village
As quietly & slowly as the limbs of some ancient oak
Growing into the upper floor windows of a house
That has been abandoned; it is the same laughter the cook hears,
Day in, day out, in the years that follow,
A laughter spreading over the village until, one day,
The cook closes his eyes, he stuffs a finger into each ear, he tries
To will the gods into something else. *But what?* he wonders,
Because he can't think of anything else,
And when he begins to see, with his eyes still closed,
The two thin spiderwebs glistening with frost & trembling
In the eaves above him, his lips are already whispering a prayer:

＊

Let them hang from some tree, let them be tatters swaying
Beneath the leaves, & let their flesh be no more to us than
The tissues of kites resting in wires or receding into the sky,
Let them be threadbare as the cold wind, & let their voices
Circle the earth in a key so high only the dogs can hear it.
For what do they amount to compared with this life
Which can do nothing else but exile you to lying awake,
Coughing, until your own blood comes out as if it wants
To say something, or is saying it, but without a mouth.
And so she heard nothing in those last moments but a boy,
A neighbor, practicing badly & without talent, over & over,
The same two notes blown through a trumpet, & then she
Realized her life would be drowned out by these two notes,
That she was this girl listening to them, that she was,
That she was with a window open & a book open on her lap,
The pages of it not yet flecked by blood as they would be.

＊

The cook felt a little strange about his prayer,
About the fury in the prayer which seemed to come
From no one, & the words of the prayer which seemed
To pass through him like words spoken by someone
Else, someone not indifferent enough to have been
A cook for all these years, to have swept out a café
With a broom in the first sun, day after day,
A place where two gods sat across from each other
In their bloody uniforms, laughing & playing cards.
So he was glad when his own thought came back to him
With the indistinguishable flavor of his voice in it;
He did not like the idea of someone else
Inside him, using words he wouldn't have used,
Though he no longer took much comfort in being glad.

＊

One day I look out & see only the empty table where the two
Of them had been sitting a moment ago & laughing. I don't think

21

Much about it; the quiet feels like someone's there, though
We're closed. O.K., so it's a Thursday. I give the dishwasher
A little something extra so he can take this girl, this
Little blonde thing who looks like she's been half erased
By life, to the movies. I give him something extra even though
She's so high all the time it must be like having, I don't know,
A date with . . . evaporation or something. I mean I can imagine
Her sitting there in the dark of the matinee as transfixed
By the shadowy creases in the curtain covering the screen
As she is by any image after it goes up. Anyway, I hope
They fuck each other's lights out right there in the balcony.
But maybe they just sit there, Orfeo with his sweaty
Palms & this little wilting thing in her platform shoes.
So I'm alone & sweeping up the place when in walks
This god we call Troppo Piccolo wearing socks flashy as
Hose on an Easter priest, & who doesn't believe me when
I tell him I'm out of the codfish, goat cheese, & sun-dried
Tomato sandwich, & won't believe me I'm also out
Of the paté de campagne. He says I'm lying. No, I tell him,
It's the geese, the ducks. They've evolved to this pure state
Where they feed on the shadows of clouds so don't need
Livers to digest with anymore, & where they multiply
So quickly & quietly they're blackening the sun; I mean,
Look how dark it is in here. Besides, I tell him, I only lie
To people I respect, or love. Cops, for example, even cops
I know, I have enough respect to lie to them. If I don't,
They've got to file a report. They hate that. The form's
As long as a mortgage. I lied to this little girl I knew who
Was coughing blood, who was turning into bloodstains right
In front of me. I told her, it's nothing. I told her she wasn't
Dying, no way you can die when you're twelve, no way you
Can die when someone is blowing a note on the trumpet, C flat,
Outside your window. I wanted her to smile. I wanted it all
To be like a scene in some forties movie where she would
Smile at the end, & forgive everything. But she didn't smile.
I don't lie to you guys who aren't even there playing cards
At your usual table. I don't respect you. I serve you
Camparis anyway & as I do I pray your dicks turn into marble
And break off & fall into the sea while you're pissing off
A cliff on your way home. By now I've chopped up two

22

Onions & a clove of garlic I'm so thrilled to get this anger
Out of me at last, & so I tell Troppo Piccolo who thinks
He's immortal, who thinks he's so much purer than the two
Slightly different moistures that composed him out of nothing
At all: Pain? Buddy you wouldn't believe the kind of pain
That little girl went through at the end. And I don't even
See it coming his hands are so fast. The last thing I see
Is this sliver of basil I've just sliced, & the long gleaming
Blade of the Sabatier knife with the black handle falling
Seriously as if I've never seen it before for the kind of thing
It is without me holding it, the butter just beginning to
Simmer & clarify in the small gleaming pan as I go down.

꩜

When the cook wakes on the floor, it is
Completely dark. He hears a ringing but it is in a town
Without bells.
He thinks it is black inside his skull & he is unaccountably
Happy for a few seconds to know this,
To know that, all the while, it had been only an endless
Ribbon of black air, that whirring they call *thought* that made
The lights come on softly at dusk in the cities,
And made the mall where he selected the kind of lingerie he knew
She would like, & the ingredients
He memorized for Cassoulet Houquard, Tangine à la Macaress;
That let him memorize her face for fifteen years until,
One day, he could not call
It up again; that made him solemnly promise himself
That one day
He would remember an afternoon in childhood
When he cleaned clams with a tiny brush for hours in Marseilles,
And was paid five *centimes* for it;
That let him remember how
The Sibyl from Cumae, who, granted eternal life, became so tiny—
Because her bones shrank, because she had forgotten to ask as well
For eternal youth—that they had to put her into a bird cage
On a side street just off Omonios Square to protect her
From pedestrians, so that the boys of Athens
Rattled its bars with sticks as they ran past in the centuries

Before she became gradually invisible
And someone finally threw the cage itself out;
And lets him remember
The gypsy boy playing finger cymbals in the park at dusk; the day
The girl's blood blackened the entire pillowcase;
The way the guy's punch caught him on the soft swell
Of the temple just above the ear; the smells
Of fish & lemons & the wet streets in the mornings all swirling
Together in the way thoughts continue to swirl
For a few seconds even in someone who suddenly slumps again
Though it seems to him he must
Still be quietly standing, in the idea of himself, in the dignity of it,
And the indignity of it,
In the dark kitchen of a café he once owned.

After the guy's gone out, it's quiet enough in the place
To hear the goddess whispering in my ear again. She isn't
Wearing anything. She's just standing naked beside me.
I keep stirring two eggs into a sauce that's been simmering
Maybe an hour by now. I can't see her but I know she's there.
She's invisible in the soft light of the afternoon; as she
Keeps whispering in my ear the first leaves unfurl
Along the roadsides south of town, & then the hazy green
Of spring begins to come back on the streets outside. She
Keeps whispering, & soon the thick leaves of summer crowd
The city, & darken the boulevards & the traffic passing under
Them, the leaves keep listening for something that isn't
There yet. It's so still I can't hear anything except what
She's whispering. I'm nodding by now & crying silently
Above the hot stove because I understand every word
She's whispering. I feel stupid turning the burner off
Because I'm not even in this world anymore when I do this,
And do it anyway more out of habit than anything else,
I guess, but it won't turn off, the flame keeps burning,
So I take the saucepan off the burner & throw it against
The wall to hear the clamor that it makes, but when I look up
Nothing has happened; the cold, gleaming circles of pots,
Pans, & chafing dishes are all in their places along the wall

So undisturbed they might as well have been nothing more
Than leaves in moonlight all those years I used them & knew
Them better than I knew anyone. She's whispering something
Else to me now, something different, & when I hear it clearly
I turn to the empty darkness of the kitchen & say to no one
At all, to the great Unlistening No One called the World, I say:
You can shove this kitchen up your ass, & then I take off my apron
As easily as I always have, I take off my apron & let it fall
To the floor. I put my arm in her arm, & I begin to walk out
Of this small cage that did not know it was a cage, I walk out
Of it for the last time, I begin walking out of it forever,
Orfeo already bending over my body with his ear against
My chest. The first step feels like air taking a step into air.
And the next does too, though I ascend a little this time.
I realize I am nothing more now than air rising silently
And crying silently & I don't want to cry—it's not something
You want to see, air crying as it rises, so I hesitate
For a moment, my vanished eyes already dry
Even as I turn back for a last look: Orfeo, I say to him,
Though he can't hear me, turn off the radio as you go out,
Don't be in any big hurry to get married, & boil the spoons
If they're greasy, like you want to teach them a lesson.
And it's only in this moment I realize how ridiculous
My voice sounds as it rings & rings in this empty kitchen,
Though for years I held it out to others, like an oar; I knew
The river beside the village was still, the village floated.
When I mentioned this once to Orfeo, he nodded, but didn't
Look up from scrubbing the fried eggplant from a pan.
The way he didn't look up is the way the village overflowed,
Lost its way, became the sound of traffic on a boulevard.
You'd never know it was there. And those two guys in their
Blood-stained uniforms? They can't even get a table now.
They've been waiting beside the coat rack for so long
They seem like part of the decor, like something in the wallpaper,
Like a deck of cards spilling from the window of a train,
Like the shaky letters Orfeo squeezes onto birthday cakes.

The Smell of the Sea

Because they could not blind him twice, they drove a pencil
Through the blind king's ear. The pencil could not believe the thing
It had been asked to do, but by then it was already entering the mind,

And there it forgot that it had ever been a pencil.

Darkness reigned in the basement of the record store in Ogden, Utah,
Where all this happened, & there wasn't any king. The other king, the one who
Came in the night, was blind & mad, & owned a record store. And was a Mormon.

So were his ungrateful daughters who would pretend to pry his eyes out
With kitchen spoons, & so, within the kingdom, was everyone except
The Fool who repaired chainsaws & snowmobiles & thought of them as small,

Snarling gods whose faith & hatred of trees was perfect. The man who owned

the record store had once suspected God did not exist & had spent a summer
Lying on the beach at Santa Monica trying hard not to believe in God,
And was unable to. It was 1967. *Wild Thing* was coming from a radio. Her name

Was Dawn. She had dropped a half tab of acid an hour before he picked her up,
And didn't say a word until they were driving back & then she said "Blue lights . . .
So many blue lights." "Yeah, well, it's the airport. We're driving by the airport now,"

He explained. "Oh," she said. Maybe it was the acid that had made her seem

As distant & withdrawn as the world was, stretched across a quiet evening.
Where was *Wild Thing?* Dawn was hazy, overcast, & about as much
Fun to be with as the third wife at the wedding of a Spanish Fork polygamist.

The woman in her hopeless gingham dress had looked on, smiled at her husband,
Then at the teenage bride. "You kin to her?" she had asked him. He had come
With a friend who thought the whole thing would be amusing, he had no idea who

The girl was. "That little slut?" he had wanted to say because he wanted to say

Something shocking. He still wanted to until the woman turned to him & said,
"With so many people showin' up, we're stretching it pretty thin. But we got chili
    dogs
And ice cream anyway. We splurged." The way someone had carefully trimmed
The yard with its small, parched lawn, & strung balloons on a clothesline, suddenly
Filled him with pity. Faith showed itself in the rib cage. Its bones were visible.
He could see them beneath the too-small bodice of the woman's dress.

Faith resided there, under the shriveled & lost left nipple.

He liked music. He liked hearing it while he worked.

And now he owned the store, although, for an hour or two each night,
He was both blind & mad & believed in kings. And believed he was a king,
And it never once entered his mind that the pencil balanced between

The pulse of his temple & his ear had been invented long after the deaths of kings.
After they had done the scene, he would remember who he was again,
An ordinary man who knew it & would have been insane because of knowing it

If he could not crawl toward Dover on his knees. He couldn't act.

When he dressed in weeds, his Temple garment showed under them.
One day he pretended he was a king who had disguised himself as the owner
Of a record store. The king sold eighteen new Donny & Maries before

He abdicated his vinyl throne & went home. If he fell from a high place it would be
A canyon wall he thought he remembered well enough to climb alone.
The water in the stream beneath him would wrinkle & whiten over the rocks as it

Always had & the trees rushing toward him would show him only that they could not

Help it. He knew who he was. Someone would ask him whether he carried
Brahms' *German Requiem*, or Valery Wellington on an extinct Chicago blues label,
And he had both. Sometimes he was sick of who he was, & the sickness passed.
The two guys who came in that afternoon were AWOL from a nearby army base,

And maybe only intended to rob the place, & had no idea who they were.
There was a young woman who worked afternoons there & her boyfriend had

Stopped by to tease & flirt with her a little. The two men pretended to browse

Through the stacks of record albums for a while, & then made the owner close
The store & marched them down the steps, & made the woman take off her dress,
And made the boyfriend watch as one, & then the other, raped her there.

What happened after that is blind & smells its way to the sea. They forced
The woman & her boyfriend to swallow some Drano from a can, & then flushed
Their mouths with water & made them swallow. But before they found the leftover
    can

With the snowy crystals in it, or had thought of using it,

One of them must have noticed the owner with the pencil in his ear, then
the short pine two-by-four. "Has the thought ever entered your mind . . . ?"
One of them said after they had made the man lie on the floor, made him lie on his
    side

With his ear exposed, with his ear turned up to them, listening to everything,
Wondering how an ear could feel naked when it never had before. Did the man
    really
Believe the two of them would let the others live if he would lie as still as possible,
    as they

Had told him to, & let them do it?

This is usually the moment when the Fool is hanged & the poet disappears because
He doesn't know what happens next & a hunger with a mouth as small as the eye
Of a sewing needle overruns & darkens the flaxen grasses & the willows & the staring
Eyes of ponds, & you know there wasn't any king. There was only a man who owned
A record store & who believed two murderers would be kind, & keep their promises,
And waited for it to happen, lying there on his side, waiting until they were ready to
    drive

The unbelieving pencil through his ear.

Elegy with a Petty Thief in the Rigging

That afternoon after he found it,
The music of a keel scrape still in his ears,

Columbus wrote in a journal: "Walking under the trees there
Was the most beautiful thing

I have ever seen." It's what he left out of it, out
Of the entry, that looks back in recognition.

Did he mean walking there? Did he mean the empty, shaded
Spaces beneath the trees where he rested

After sending his men off to accomplish some task?
To find a waterfall & a China behind it?

Did he mean someone he saw?

But the entire point of the entry, the impossible
Chore he had assigned the men,

Was to be left alone there,

With the sky washed clean above him, with the sun
Burning through all its likenesses

To be what it is, by erasing them.

❧

Ecstasy, in the original sense, meant rapture,
Meant standing outside oneself.

If that is what it was,

If he walked beside himself there on the path that led
To the New World, how long

Can it have lasted, & at what point
Did the sunlight weaken on the path & the men come back,

And with them the hollow sound of the wave chop on the hull
And then the whitecaps appearing

And disappearing, & then maps, riggings, finitude, a crust
Of bread left on a cabin sill, & beyond

The porthole & the wheel the sea shattering the sea
Into air, into the shattered, reforming

Sea & sky again, & then into harbors, wharves,
The ancient walls of cities, moats & courtyards & asylums,

And the sun taking its place again in a stained-glass window
As if someone had decreed it so by law, drawn up

In Latin the exact angle of its light?

And the one who saw the place for the first time

While the wind was unblessing the sails, the boy
In the crow's nest, the thief up there,

Paroled from prison by the queen & expecting
The world to end

In one unending fall of water, who watches carefully,
Who keeps the actual feel of rope

In his hand, holds it there until one day he sees

A twig on a small wave, & then another, then
The soaked black curl of bark, & its

Pale underside, & then the first bird, & then
Another, & another?

And me sitting up there with him, invisible,
Beside him in the rigging,

Thinking that if this is the story
The two of us

Are no more significant to it than whitecaps
Far out at sea,

That paradise would make either one of us
Long for a bar with a good pool table,

A beach town, & a rain without end?

And this kid, fifteen years old,
The first to glimpse the New World? He's not saying

A word about it yet,

He's just sitting here, watching a coastline begin
To take a shape.

Let me move to one side so you can hear his thought
Without me in it anymore:

❧

"First thing I'm gonna do is kill Supedas,
Then I'm gonna chop off his hand & boil it

Until my ring falls off. If you help me, Jesus,
Maybe it could be a little bit your ring, too,

But I'm the one who gets to wear it from now on."

And the coastline gradually getting larger
From where I sit, the boy beside me planning

What might be, for all I know, the first murder

In the New World, its wilderness spreading
Over his expressionless face? I'm glad

It's not a story.

Elegy for Whatever Had a Pattern in It

1

Now that the Summer of Love has become the moss of tunnels
And the shadowy mouths of tunnels & all the tunnels lead into the city,

I'm going to put the one largely forgotten, swaying figure of Ediesto Huerta
Right in front of you so you can watch him swamp fruit

Out of an orchard in the heat of an August afternoon, I'm going to let you

Keep your eyes on him as he lifts & swings fifty-pound boxes of late
Elberta peaches up to me where I'm standing on a flatbed trailer & breathing in
Tractor exhaust so thick it bends the air, bends things seen through it

So that they seem to swim through the air.

It is a lousy job, & no one has to do it, & we do it.

We do it so that I can show you even what isn't there,
What's hidden. And signed by Time itself. And set spinning,

And is only a spider, after all, with its net waiting for what falls,
For what flies into it, & ages, & turns gray in a matter of minutes. The web
Is nothing's blueprint, bleached by the sun & whitened by it, it's what's left

After we've vanished, after we become what falls apart when anyone

Touches it, eyelash & collarbone dissolving into air, & time touching
The boxes we are wrapped in like gifts & splintering them

Into wood again, at the edge of a wood.

2

Black Widow is a name no one ever tinkered with or tried to change.
If you turn her on her back you can see the blood red hourglass figure

She carries on her belly,

Small as the design of a pirate I saw once on a tab of blotter acid

33

Before I took half of it, & a friend took the other, & then the two of us
Walked down to the empty post office beside the lake to look,

For some reason, at the wanted posters. We liked a little drama
In the ordinary then. Now a spider's enough.

And this one, in the legend she inhabits, is famous, & the male dies.
She eats its head after the eggs are fertilized.

It's the hourglass on her belly I remember, & the way the figure of it,
Figure eight of Time & Infinity, looked like something designed,

Etched or embossed upon the slick undershell, & the way there was,
The first time I saw it, a stillness in the pattern that was not
The stillness of the leaves or the stillness of the sky over the leaves.

After the male dies she goes off & the eggs

Live in the fraying sail

Of an abandoned web strung up in the corner of a picking box or beneath
Some slowly yellowing grape leaf among hundreds of other
Leaves, in autumn, the eggs smaller than the *o* in this typescript

Or a handwritten apostrophe in ink.

What do they represent but emptiness, some gold camp settlement
In the Sierras swept clean by smallpox, & wind?

Canal School with its three rooms, its bell & the rope you rang it with
And no one there in the empty sunlight, ring & after ring & echo.

It magnifies & I can't explain it.

Piedra, Conejo, Parlier. Stars & towns, blown fire & wind.
Deneb & Altair, invisible kindling, nothing above nothing.

It magnifies & I can't explain it.

3

Expressionless spinster, carrying Time's signature preserved & signed
In blood & hidden beneath you, you move two steps
To the right & hold still, then one step to the left,

And hold still again, motionless as the web you wait in.

Motionless as the story you wait in & inhabit but did not spin
And did not repeat. You wait in the beehive hairdo of the girl
Sitting across from me in class, wait in your eggs,

4

Wait in the hair the girl teases & sprays once more at recess.

Lipstick, heels, tight sweater, leather anklet.

The story has no point but stillness itself, absence in a school desk,
The hacked and scratched names visible in the varnished wood,

No one there, the bell with its ring & after ring & echo.

In class, I remember, she would look back at me with a gaze deeper
Than calm, blanker than a pond's scummed & motionless surface,
Beneath which there was nothing, nothing taking the shape of someone

Who had already drowned but could not die, & so sat in class
Because she had to, because that was the law.

Mrs. Avery went on & on at the blackboard so we could know
Who Magellan & Vizcaino had been, or sometimes she would make

The boy who spoke only Spanish read from a book,
Watch him as he used his forefinger to point at each syllable

He would read, read & mispronounce, & stumble over, & go on.

And this isn't much of a story either, but it's one I know:

One afternoon in August, two black widow spiders bit Ediesto Huerta.
He killed them both & went on working,

Went on swinging the boxes up to me. In a few minutes the sweat
Bathed his face until it glistened, & still he went on working;
And when I asked him to stop he would not & instead

Seemed to begin to dance slowly in the rhythms of the work,
Swing & heft & turning back for another box, then

Swing, heft, & turning back again. And within a half hour or so,
Without him resting once but merely swinging box after box

Of peaches up to me in the heat, the fever broke.

5

In the middle of turning away again, he stopped dancing,
He stopped working. He seemed to be listening to something, & then

He passed out & fell flat on his back. It looked as if he had gone to sleep
For a moment. I let the idling tractor sputter & die, & by the time

I reached him, he had awakened, &, in the next moment, his face

Began twitching, his arms & legs danced to something without music
And then stiffened, his jaws clenched & his eyes fluttered open
And turned a pure white. I made a stick from a peach limb & tore

The leaves & shoots off it & stuck it between his teeth

As I heard one was supposed to, &, in this way, almost
Killed him by suffocation, & so took the stick out & threw it away.

And later lifted him by the one arm he extended to me & pulled him up onto
The bed of the trailer. He dangled his legs off the rear of it.

We sat there, saying nothing.

It was so quiet we could hear the birds around us in the trees.

And then he turned to me, &, addressing me in a name as old as childhood,
Said, "Hey Cow*boy*, you wanna cigarette?"

❧

In the story, no one can remember whether it was car theft or burglary,
But in fact, Ediesto Huerta was tried & convicted of something, & so, afterward,
Became motionless & silent in the web spun around him by misfortune.

In the penitentiary the lights stay on forever,

Cell after cell after cell, they call their names out, caught in time.

Ring, & after ring, & echo.

In the story, the girl always dies of spider bites,
When in fact she disappeared by breaking into the jagged pieces of glass
Littering the roadsides & glinting in the empty light that shines there.

6

All we are is representation, what we appear to be & are, & are not,
And representation is all we remember,

Something hesitating & looking back & caught for a moment.

God in the design on a spider's belly, standing for time & infinity,
Looks back, looks back just once, then never again.

We go without a trace, I am thinking. We go & there's no one there,
No one to meet us on the long drive lined with orange trees,
Cypresses, the bleaching fronds of palm trees,

And though the town is still there when I return to it, when I'm gone
The track is empty beside the station, & the station is boarded up,
Boarded over, the town is overgrown with leaves, with weeds

Tall as windowsills, window glass out & dark inside the shops.

The classrooms & school are gone & the bell, & the rope
To ring it with, & the boy reading from the book, forefinger
On a syllable he can't pronounce & stumbles over again & again.

❧

All we are is representation, what we are & are not,

Clear & then going dark again, all we are
Is the design or insignia that mispresents what we are, & stays

Behind, & looks back at us without expression, empty road in sunlight
I once drove in a '48 Jimmy truck with three tons of fruit
On it & the flooring beneath the clutch so worn away I could see

The road go past beneath me, the oil flecked light & shadow

Picking up speed. Angel & Johnny Dominguez, Ediesto Huerta,
Jaime Vaca & Coronado Solares, Querido Flacco

7

And the one called Dead Rat & the one called Camelias;

We go without a trace, I am thinking.

❧

Today you were lying in bed, drinking tea, reading the newspaper,
A look of concentration on your face, of absorption in some

Story or other.

It looked so peaceful, you reading, the bed, the sunlight over everything.

There is a blueprint of something never finished, something I'll never
Find my way out of, some web where the light rocks, back & forth,
Holding me in a time that's gone, bee at the windowsill & the cold

38

Coming back as it has to, tapping at the glass.

The figure in the hourglass & the body swinging in the rhythm of its work.
The body reclining in bed, forgetting what it is, & who.

While the night goes on with its work, the stars & the shapes they make,
Cold vein in the leaf & in the wind,

What are we but what we offer up?

Gifts we give, things for oblivion to look at, & puzzle over, & set aside,

Oblivion resting his cheek against a child's striped rubber ball
In the photograph I have of him, head on the table & resting his cheek
Against the cool surface of the ball, the one that is finished spinning, the one

He won't give back.

Oblivion who has my face in the photograph, my cheek resting
Against a child's striped ball.

Oblivion with his blown fires, & empty towns . . .

Oblivion who would be nothing without us, I am thinking,

8

As if we're put on the earth to forget the ending, & wander.
And walk alone. And walk in the midst of great crowds,

And never come back.

III

Elegy with the Sprawl of a Wave Inside It

The two black swans paddling the brown canals of Sheffield Park

Are still together. The chains of their days, the bright ripples
Linked by sunlight in their passing wake,

Leave them unchanged:

Still so aloof & out of reach they shy away from the outstretched
Hands of tourists,

And weave a stillness onto the water as they pass.
The motion of their wake is a stillness.

August Sebastiani kept a pair of black squabbling swans.
He was friendly, they were not.

Grapes were selling for twenty dollars a ton.
He could afford the dislike of swans, &,

After he died, the eye of Black Swan, indifferent as instinct
Itself, looks out from the label on a Pinot Noir Blanc.

They are the kind of thing Yeats is writing about, while Dowson
Lies on his back, staring at the ceiling after

He's thrown up in the small toilet.

If I transpose all this into another key, if I inscribe
The unaware of itself

Swimming in its black plumage into . . .

But I can't.

They are more speechless than the spreading moss
On the wall above them,

And are already exaggerations.

There's stillness in their motion & motion in their stillness;

Two old hats drifting on the water.

2

The wooden streets of MacLeod are lost in snow.

I love to say the names, over & over,
For the luster of their syllables: Vizcaino & Magellan,

Drake disappearing into mist off the Farallones.

Murrieta, Sontag & Evans, the Skeleton Club,

My grandmother Adah coming home after teaching school in a buggy
Drawn by the two horses, Anastasia & Sandman,

A small Derringer with a pearl handle in her lap.

My father walking halfway over the swaying bridge
Of the last whaling boat—

Bound for Juneau out of San Francisco Bay &
Then turning around in the middle, deciding not to.

❧

At Sunset & La Cienega, one billboard displayed Philomel
With her tongue cut out, the other one a wall of flame.

As cheap paneling is speechless, & tract homes.
As flames are a speechlessness. As flames so testify.

A mile from where I was born, there was a labor camp
That housed a thousand migrant families

In chicken sheds, white leftover feathers & the stucco
Of dung still there,

With its odor of ammonia rising into the dust & spreading
Into the light & air.

It made it hard to breathe it in,

Their fingers clinging to chicken wire as they stared out,
Whole families, waiting.

What does this image mean, someone asked me once,
In Richmond, in the Commonwealth Club, the portrait of Lee

Soaring above us, bourbon & ice appearing on a silver tray—

"What was *that*, anyways?" That was 1955,

Whole families in cages.
"It was a disgrace," I answered.

❧

When I go back I feel exiled from it all.

And always there are two thoughts, one cutting through
The first until it isn't there.

Overlooking the narrow road that leads out of Porlone & the wild
Solitude of the South Coast,

Stunted pines & rock-strewn hills giving way to bleached grass,
And a longing for solitude rushing in

And replacing, a moment later, what I had thought
Was solitude—& the longing wilder

And more permanent, &,

Coming as it does in the wake of everything, the endless mimicry
In the gull's cry & the sprawl of a wave. . . .

3

They called it—what else?—*Eye of the Swan*.

It's a common wine, & tastes best when drunk
With a good friend on the pier at Eureka,

The wind turning sharper & colder as it comes in off the Pacific,
Best drunk barefoot, & dangling your legs off the old lumber

Soaked with salt & the rough spray of the surf there;
                              The present can't remember what it is.

Elegy with a Thimbleful of Water in the Cage

It's a list of what I cannot touch:

Some dandelions & black-eyed Susans growing back like innocence
Itself, with its thoughtless style,

Over an abandoned labor camp south of Piedra;

And the oldest trees, in that part of Paris with a name I forget,
Propped up with sticks to keep their limbs from cracking,

And beneath such quiet, a woman with a cane,

And knowing, if I came back, I could not find them again;

And a cat I remember who slept on the burnished mahogany
In the scooped-out beveled place on the counter below

The iron grillwork, the way you had to pass your letter *over* him
As he slept through those warm afternoons

In New Hampshire, the gray fur stirring a little as he inhaled;

The small rural post office growing smaller, then lost, tucked
Into the shoreline of the lake when I looked back;

Country music from a lone radio in an orchard there.
The first frost already on the ground.

❧

And those who slipped out of their names, as if *called*
Out of them, as if they had been waiting

To be called:

Stavros lecturing from his bequeathed chair at the Café Midi,
In the old Tower Theatre District, his unending solo

Above the traffic on Olive, asking if we knew what happened
To the Sibyl at Cumae *after* Ovid had told her story,

After Petronius had swept the grains of sand from it, how,

Granted eternal life, she had forgotten to ask for youth, & so,
As she kept aging, as her body shrank within itself

And the centuries passed, she finally

Became so tiny they had to put her into a jar, at which point
Petronius lost track of her, lost interest in her,

And at which point she began to suffocate

In the jar, suffocate without being able to die, until, finally,
A Phoenician sailor slipped the gray piece of pottery—

Its hue like an overcast sky & revealing even less—

Into his pocket, & sold it on the docks at Piraeus to a shop owner
Who, hearing her gasp, placed her in a birdcage

On a side street just off Onmonios Square, not to possess her,

But to protect her from pedestrians, & the boys of Athens rattled
The bars of her cage with sticks as they ran past yelling,

"Sibyl, Sibyl, what do you want?"—each generation having to
Listen more closely than the one before it to hear

The faintest whispered rasp from the small bitter seed
Of her tongue as she answered them with the same

Remark passing through time, "I want to die!" As time passed & she
Gradually grew invisible, the boys had to press

Their ears against the cage to hear her.

And then one day the voice became too faint, no one could hear it,
And after that they stopped telling

The story. And then it wasn't a story, it was only an empty cage.
That hung outside a shop among the increasing

Noise of traffic, &, from the square itself, blaring from loudspeakers,
The shattered glass & bread of political speeches

That went on half the night, & the intermittent music of strip shows
In summer when the doors of the bars were left open,

And then, Stavros said, the sun shone straight through the cage.

You could see there was nothing inside it, he said, unless you noticed
How one of the little perches swung back & forth, almost

Imperceptibly there, though the street was hot, windless; or unless
You thought you saw a trace of something flicker across

The small mirror above the thimbleful of water, which of course
Shouldn't have been there, which should have evaporated

Like the voice that went on whispering ceaselessly its dry rage

Without listeners. He said that even if anyone heard it,
They could not have recognized the dialect

As anything human.

He would lie awake, the only boy in Athens who

Still heard it repeating its wish to die, & he was not surprised,
He said, when the streets, the bars & strip shows,

Began to fill with German officers, or when the loudspeakers
And the small platform in the square were, one day,

Shattered into a thousand pieces.

As the years passed, as even the sunlight began to seem
As if it was listening to him outside the windows

Of the Midi, he began to lose interest in stories, & to speak
Only in abstractions, to speak only of theories,

Never of things.

Then he began to come in less frequently, & when he did,
He no longer spoke at all. And so,

Along the boulevards in the winter the bare limbs of the trees
One passed in the city became again

Only the bare limbs of trees; no girl stepped into them
To tell us of their stillness. We would hear

Rumors of Stavros following the gypsy Pentecostalists into
Their tents, accounts of him speaking in tongues;

Glossolalia, he once said, which was all speech, & none.

In a way, it didn't matter anymore. Something in time was fading—
And though girls still came to the café to flirt or argue politics

Or buy drugs from the two ancient boys expressionless as lizards
Now as they bent above a chessboard—

By summer the city parks had grown dangerous.

No one went there anymore to drink wine, dance, & listen
To metal amplified until it seemed, as it had

Seemed once, the bitter, cleansing angel released at last from what
Fettered it inside us. And maybe there

Wasn't any angel after all. The times had changed. It became
Difficult to tell for sure. And anyway,

There was a law against it now; a law against gathering at night
In the parks was actually all that the law

Said was forbidden for us to do, but it came to the same thing.
It meant you were no longer permitted to know,

Or to decide for yourself,

Whether there was an angel inside you, or whether there wasn't.

෴

Poverty is what happens at the end of any story, including this one,
When there are too many stories.

When you can believe in all of them, & so believe in none;
When one condition is as good as any other.

The swirl of wood grain in this desk: is it the face of an angel, or
The photograph of a girl, the only widow in her high school,

After she has decided to turn herself

Into a tree? (It was a rainy afternoon, & her van skidded at sixty;
For a split second the trunk of an oak had never seemed

So solemn as it did then, widening before her.)

Or is it misfortune itself, or the little grimace the woman
Makes with her mouth above the cane,

There, then not there, then there again?

Or is it the place where the comparisons, the little comforts
Like the cane she's leaning on, give way beneath us?

෴

What do you do when nothing calls you anymore?
When you turn & there is only the light filling the empty window?

When the angel fasting inside you has grown so thin it flies
Out of you a last time without your

Knowing it, & the water dries up in its thimble, & the one swing
In the cage comes to rest after its almost imperceptible,

Almost endless, swaying?

I'm going to stare at the whorled grain of wood in this desk
I'm bent over until it's infinite,

I'm going to make it talk, I'm going to make it
Confess everything.

I was about to ask you if you were cold, if you wanted a sweater,
Because . . . well, as Stavros would say

Before he began one of those

Stories that seemed endless, the sun pressing against
The windows of the café & glinting off the stalled traffic

Just beyond them, this could take a while;

❧

I pass the letter I wrote to you over the sleeping cat & beyond

the iron grillwork, into the irretrievable.

Elegy with a Bridle in Its Hand

One was a bay cowhorse from Piedra & the other was a washed-out palomino
And both stood at the rail of the corral & both went on aging
In each effortless tail swish, the flies rising, then congregating again

Around their eyes & muzzles & withers.

Their front teeth were by now yellow as antique piano keys & slanted to the angle
Of shingles on the maze of sheds & barn around them; their puckered

Chins were round & black as frostbitten oranges hanging unpicked from the limbs
Of trees all through winter like a comment of winter itself on everything
That led to it & found gradually the way out again.

In the slowness of time. Black time to white, & rind to blossom.
Deity is in the details & we are details among other details & we long to be

Teased out of ourselves. And become all of them.

The bay had worms once & had acquired the habit of drinking orange soda
From an uptilted bottle & nibbling cookies from the flat of a hand, & liked to do
Nothing else now, & the palomino liked to do nothing but gaze off

At traffic going past on the road beyond vineyards & it would follow each car
With a slight turning of its neck, back & forth, as if it were a thing

Of great interest to him.

If I rode them, the palomino would stumble & wheeze when it broke
Into a trot & would relapse into a walk after a second or two & then stop
Completely & without cause; the bay would keep going though it creaked

Underneath me like a rocking chair of dry, frail wood, & when I knew it could no
    longer
Continue but did so anyway, or when the palomino would stop & then take

Only a step or two when I nudged it forward again, I would slip off either one of
    them,
Riding bareback, & walk them slowly back, letting them pause when they wanted to.

At dawn in winter sometimes there would be a pane of black ice covering
The surface of the water trough & they would nudge it with their noses or muzzles,
And stare at it as if they were capable of wonder or bewilderment.

They were worthless. They were the motionless dusk & the motionless

Moonlight, & in the moonlight they were other worlds. Worlds uninhabited
And without visitors. Worlds that would cock an ear a moment
When the migrant workers come back at night to the sheds they were housed in

And turn a radio on, but only for a moment before going back to whatever

Wordless & tuneless preoccupation involved them.

The palomino was called Misfit & the bay was named Querido Flacco,
And the names of some of the other shapes had been Rockabye
And Ojo Pendejo & Cue Ball & Back Door Peter & Frenchfry & Sandman

And Rolling Ghost & Anastasia.

Death would come for both of them with its bridle of clear water in hand
And they would not look up from grazing on some patch of dry grass or even

Acknowledge it much; & for a while I began to think that the world

Rested on a limitless ossuary of horses where their bones & skulls stretched
And fused until only the skeleton of one enormous horse underlay
The smoke of cities & the cold branches of trees & the distant

Whine of traffic on the interstate.

If I & by implication therefore anyone looked at them long enough at dusk
Or in moonlight he would know the idea of heaven & of life everlasting
Was so much blown straw or momentary confetti

At the unhappy wedding of a sister.

Heaven was neither the light nor was it the air, & if it took a physical form
It was splintered lumber no one could build anything with.

54

Heaven was a weight behind the eyes & one would have to stare right through it
Until he saw the air itself, just air, the clarity that took the shackles from his eyes
And the taste of the bit from his mouth & knocked the rider off his back

So he could walk for once in his life.

Or just stand there for a moment before he became something else, some
Flyspeck on the wall of a passing & uninterruptible history whose sounds claimed
To be a cheering from bleachers but were actually no more than the noise

Of cars entering the mouth of a tunnel.

And in the years that followed he would watch them in the backstretch or the far
    turn
At Santa Anita or Del Mar. Watch the way they made it all seem effortless,

Watch the way they were explosive & untiring.

And then watch the sun fail him again & slip from the world, & watch
The stands slowly empty. As if all moments came back to this one, inexplicably
To this one out of all he might have chosen—Heaven with ashes in its hair

And filling what were once its eyes—this one with its torn tickets
Littering the aisles & the soft racket the wind made. This one. Which was his.

And if the voice of a broken king were to come in the dusk & whisper
To the world, that grandstand with its thousands of empty seats,

Who among the numberless you have become desires this moment

Which comprehends nothing more than loss & fragility & the fleeing of flesh?
He would have to look up at quickening dark & say: *Me. I do. It's mine.*

Elegy for Poe with the Music of a Carnival Inside It

There is this sunny place where I imagine him.
A park on a hill whose grass wants to turn
Into dust, & would do so if it weren't
For the rain, & the fact that it is only grass
That keeps the park from flowing downhill past
Its trees & past the slender figures in the statues.
Their stone blends in with the sky when the sky
Is overcast. The stone is a kind of rain,
And half the soldiers trapped inside the stone
Are dead. The others have deserted & run home.
At this time in the morning, half sun, half mist,
There are usually three or four guys sprawled
Alone on benches facing away from one another.
If they're awake, they look as if they haven't slept.
If they're asleep, they look as if they may not wake . . .
I only imagine it as a sunny place. If they're
Awake, they gaze off as if onto a distant landscape,
Not at the warehouses & the freeway the hill overlooks,
Not onto Jefferson Avenue where, later, they'll try
To score a little infinity wrapped up in tinfoil,
Or a flake of heaven tied up in a plastic bag
And small as their lives are now, but at a city
That is not the real city gradually appearing
As the mist evaporates. For in the real city,
One was kicked in the ribs by a night watchman
Until he couldn't move. Another was
A small-time dealer until he lost his nerve
And would then have become a car thief, if only
The car had started. And the last failed to appear,
Not only for a court date, but for life itself.
In these ways, they are like Poe if Poe had lived
Beyond composing anything, & had been kicked to death
And then dismembered in this park, his limbs
Thrown as far away from what was left of him
As they could be thrown. And they are not like Poe.
The three of them stare off at a city that is there
In the distance, where they are loved for no
Clear reason, a city they walk toward when
They are themselves again, a city
That vanishes each morning in the pale light.

Poe would have admired them, & pitied them.
For Poe detested both the real city with its traffic
Crawling over the bridges, & the city that vanishes.

In autumn the rain slants & flesh turns white.
The tents go up again on the edge of town, &,
In the Carny's spiel, everyone gets lost,
And Poe, dismembered, becomes no more than the moral
In the story of his life, the cautionary tale
No better than the sideshow where the boy
With sow's hoofs instead of hands, taps the glass—
Some passing entertainment for the masses.
In the carny's spiel, everyone lost comes
Back again. Even Poe comes back to see
Himself, disfigured, in another. That is what
He's doing here, longing to mingle, invisibly,
With the others on the crowded midway as they lick
Their cotton candy, & stare expressionlessly
At one another. He wants to see the woman
Who has fins instead of arms, & the man without
A mouth. He wants to see the boy behind glass
And his own clear reflection in the glass.
The carnival's so close, only a few blocks,
That he can hear the intermittent off-key music
Wheezing faintly out of the merry-go-round . . .
It might as well be music from the moon.
The traffic never lets him cross. The weeks pass,
And then the months, & then the years with their wars
And the marquees going blank above the streets
Because no one comes anymore. And the crowd,
Filing into the little tent, watches suspiciously,
For the crowd believes in nothing now but disbelief.
And therefore, at the intersection of radiance
And death, the intersection of the real city
And the one that vanishes, Poe is pausing
In the midst of traffic, one city inside the other.
The rain slants. The flesh is a white dust.
The cars pass slowly through him, & the boy keeps
Tapping at the glass, unable to tell his story.

Elegy with an Angel at Its Gate

1. Muir in the Wilderness

We were the uncountable stars, at first.
We were nothing at first, and the light
of what was already over still in it.

We were never the color-blind grasses,

We were never the pattern of the snake
Fading into the pattern of the leaves,
Never the empty clarity one glimpses

In water falling, in water spreading itself
Into the thin white veil of what is never there,
The moment clear and empty as a heaven

Someone has just finished sweeping

Before the moment clouds over and again
Becomes only an endless falling of water
Onto stone, and falls roaring in the ears

Until they ring, and the throat suddenly
Swollen with the eucharist of failure,
A host invisible and present everywhere,

Or, anyway, present everywhere we are.

And one by one we vanished from the place,
Vanished from it by becoming part
Of everyone, part of the horses bending

Their necks to graze, part of every law,
Part of each Apache heirloom for sale
In a window, part of the wedding cake,

Part of the smallpox epidemic, part of God,
Part of each blind crossroad, part
Of the unending rain turning to snow,

Part of each straw in the lighted,
Open doors of boxcars as they pass,
Part of the wars, part of each silk piece

Of lingerie, part of what can never be
Untangled, evaluated, cross-examined, part
Of the drive by, part of the young woman

Brushing her hair, part of the lover,
Part of the tenderest parting of flesh,
Part of what must part flesh forever,

And part of what holds it together,
Part of each one watching, with an open
Mouth, the movie at the drive-in, part

of the slaughterhouse with its fly-covered
Windows, part of the scent of linen, part
of what holds the limbs of the oldest trees

Up and out through summer after summer,
Part of the fork in the road where we took
Both directions at once to disappear in them,

Into the noise that cut us in half, part
Of the noise, part of what doesn't come back,

❧

Indifferent dog, indifferent horse, indifferent

Fly riding its back beneath the trees,
Led by the indifferent stable boy who hates
The girl who rides the horse because she's

Rich, because he reads Marx by candlelight,
Is in love with her, is leaving tomorrow
To harvest sugarcane in Cuba, is a part

Of a part of a vast revolution, of an age
Of revolutions that will free him, free us,
Free everyone, put all of us to one side,

To be part of another, larger thing that ends
By becoming a movie about it, the popcorn,
The audience sitting there watching it

With their mouths open, the big screen there
In front of them, each one a part of it
Designed to stroll languidly out

Into the hot, impossible evening in the city,
Where the signs that flash on and off above
The stores, reflected in windows and off the cars,

Resemble the piping on the ushers' uniforms.

2. *Bunny Mayo in the New World*

We brought the shape of the angel with us
In the shapes of women and in the shapes
of ships because we trusted only what we

Could feel by hand, beneath us and above us.
And sure some among us had seen angels,
In the blacksmith's empty fire in the street

With no one there. And sure someone felt an angel
In the shape of the mad daisy the hammer
In his hand became before he was emancipated

From his troubles and his flesh was left hanging
From limbs of trees and little gateposts
In the rain—as a lesson to us all—

The kind of thing the British made us memorize,
Generation after generation after generation
Until it was knowledge not worth the knowing.

Larry Doyle touched an angel once, he said,
In the woods, and said its back was thick,
Thick and fat and flat. And look at what

Happened to your Larry Doyle at the end,
Gone to hell in an Easter Basket with
Your permission, Mrs. Munna Mayo.

We was just two tents of flesh over bones.
Still, it was a surprise how easy it was
To leave the place on a warm spring afternoon,

And clatter over these long planks into
The ship with its hull shaped like famine itself,
Angel and woman and famine taking the same shape

And crowding one another in and out of it.
To follow the path those shapes kept
Disappearing on, I knew where that led,

I'd seen asylums grazing the sides of hills.
More of 'em around the City every day.
You see an angel in a bar in North Beach Love

You keep your cake hole shut about it.
Remember, a lie here and there is a veniality,
Forgettable and necessary as sin unless

You've become overattached to your state
of unemployment and think there's a sandwich
Under every pillow; otherwise, where it says

Experience on the application, you're better off
Letting your imagination fill in the blank.
But seeing things is a another matter altogether.

Here in the Sunset it is. It's not allowed.

3. Stevens

This was one idea, like water seen through glass,
Then like a water seen through completely,
Seen through and regretted and longed for

In a downpour in Hartford where he sat,
Piano and attorney of the soul, turning
Angels into air, the air into a mirror

Reflecting everything and the nothing
In everything, so that when he dozes off
In the chair, the manicurist bent over

His nails, filing them, the sound of the file
Is the sound he made as a boy, running
Over the dry beach grass on a winter day,

One step ahead of the quiet, one step ahead
Of what is overtaking him, the background chorus
Of semis on the interstate, and their new god,

Shirtless and asleep in the trailer parks,
The treeless slums on the outskirts of the slums
With trees in them, trees the past stuck there?

But he's just a man asleep. He could easily be
The pages of the newspaper spreading around him
In the yard, he could easily have been

No more than the illiterate light of a warm
Afternoon in winter shining at that moment
In which I suspended all my judgments

Of this place, because they were not mine.
But have it your way, for there wasn't any us,
There was only the empty light and a path

Running beneath the trees with no one on it,
No sound of a keel scraping the sand
of some New World, no coinage of what's sexual.

The new god is a revolver in the sun.

4. *Like the Scattered Beads of a Dime Store Rosary*

One August afternoon, in the midst of lying
To my counselor to get things over with,
The counselor appointed by the court,

A nice enough young guy with a cold,
Too many cases, and stains on his shirt,
I thought of him, of how the whole point

Was not to be trapped by circumstances,
Not to spend a night in jail in a Day-Glo
Orange jumpsuit, and then walk home past

Houses flaking into paint, into the pieces
of some puzzle the children have abandoned,
Each lighted porch a history of desolation.

The point is to live beyond all jurisdiction,
To be the uncountable stars again, the shape
Of the animal running through tall grasses.

It is too late for either of us now.
Angel in the gate, walk with me sometimes,

Or whatever it is you do, air stepping
or gliding through air, as far as you want,
As far as eternity is, in our poor neighborhood,

With the toys spreading over the lawns behind you,
And the children gone, and the sills they leaned
Out of, once . . . thin, dry, freckled as leaves,

And framed by a house that is too delicate now,
Too brittle to withstand the lightest touch,
Or any mere kingdom's nowhere breath,

With the light coming back to one star
In the late summer dusk after another
Until at last the sky above it resembles

The vast rigging of some lighted ship
Drifting slowly out of reach. Come with me,
Stray a little from your task, which is set

In stone, where you must stare out, stupidly
Pretentious, with your frown and Roman hairstyle,
And with ears that might double as handles;

Walk with me a little, just for company,
As far as your owner allows, or as far as you
Want, in our poor neighborhood; be the air

Cutting through an empty world of air,
Be the cold air of an angel, older, thinner
Than fire, like something almost remembered

From a childhood swept clean by fire,
Spreading its wise chill over my flesh
Until my flesh is my own and not my own;

For a moment, and then for one more moment,
Let me belong to another; let me step
From the snare, the lie, the trap

That would have me believe only the empty scrape
Of a man's steps as he walks home,
As he begins to hear that sound and no other,

Begins to hear, in the ancient trees he passes,
Only the echoing of his steps;
If only for the company, walk with me a little

Through the litter and catcalls of this place.

With the wrong, other angel trapped in stone,
With the heaven behind you on fire,

So that I might recognize my own voice
When no one speaks, so that I might know
Who touches me in that realm where fingers

Are extinct and no one's there, the place
This one with its trees once whispered of,
Once granted us, gave us a path to

That ran under the trees and the infinite
Whispering of what we really desired,
The dry, white path empty under the leaves

As we turned from it, and walked back
To the ship with the silly carving of the body
On its bow, and lost the place—

Lost it forever in a matter of a few seconds—
So that its melody might run through my limbs,
And loosen them, a lovely dust,

And sunlight through the windows of other lovers—
As yet unborn, their faces pressed against
The windows of the cells in the rush of the blood

Like faces pressed against the windows of a train—

Walk a few steps more with me,

Show me the house I must still be living in,
Where eternity was no more than my hand
Scurrying across a sheet of paper,

Kindling blent to the music of its hush;
Walk with me a little way past it, now,
With the wrong, other angel trapped in stone,

With the heavens behind you on fire.

Elegy with a Chimneysweep Falling Inside It

Those twenty-six letters filling the blackboard
Compose the dark, compose
The illiterate summer sky & its stars as they appear

One by one, above the schoolyard.

If the soul had a written history, nothing would have happened:
A bird would still be riding the back of a horse,

And the horse would go on grazing in a field, & the gleaners,

At one with the land, the wind, the sun examining
Their faces, would go on working,

Each moment forgotten in the swipe of a scythe.

But the walls of the labyrinth have already acquired
Their rose tint from the blood of slaves
Crushed into the stone used to build them, & the windows

Of stained glass are held in place by the shriek

And sighing body of a falling chimneysweep through
The baked & blackened air. This ash was once a village,

That snowflake, time itself.

But until the day it is permitted to curl up in a doorway,
And try to sleep, the snow falling just beyond it,

There's nothing for it to do:

The soul rests its head in its hands & stares out
From its desk at the trash-littered schoolyard,

It stays where it was left.
When the window fills with pain, the soul bears witness,
But it doesn't write. Nor does it write home,

Having no need to, having no home.
In this way, & in no other

Was the soul gradually replaced by the tens of thousands
Of things meant to represent it—

All of which proclaimed, or else lamented, its absence.

Until, in the drone of auditoriums & lecture halls, it became
No more than the scraping of a branch
Against the side of a house, no more than the wincing

Of a patient on a couch, or the pinched, nasal tenor
Of the strung-out addict's voice,

While this sound of scratching, this tapping all night,
Enlarging the quiet instead of making a music within it,

Is just a way of joining one thing to another,

Myself to whoever it is—sitting there in the schoolroom,

Sitting there while also being led through the schoolyard
Where prisoners are exercising in the cold light—

A way of joining or trying to join one thing to another,
So that the stillness of the clouds & the sky

Opening beneath the blindfold of the prisoner, & the cop
Who leads him toward it, toward the blank

Sail of the sky at the end of the world, are bewildered

So that everything, in this moment, bewilders

Them: the odd gentleness each feels in the hand
Of the other, & how they don't stop walking, not now,

Not for anything.

Elegy Ending in the Sound of a Skipping Rope

All I have left of that country is this torn scrap
Of engraved lunacy, worth less now

Than it was then, for then it was worth nothing,
Or nothing more than

The dust a wren bathes in,

The fountain dry in the park off the Zeleni Venac,
The needles of the pines dry above it,

The green shutters of the fruitsellers' stands closed
For the afternoon so that in the quiet it seemed

The wren was the only thing moving in the whole city
As it beat its wings against the stone

To rid itself of lice as the dust rose around it.

The sound of its wings, I remember, was like the sound
Of cards being shuffled, as repetitive

And as pointless.

The characters met on faint blue paper.
They were thin as paper then.

They must be starving now.

❧

I don't feel like explaining it,
And now I have to.

To illustrate its money, the State put lovers on the money,

Peasants or factory workers staring off at something
You couldn't see, something beyond them,

Something that wasn't Titograd.
They kept looking at it with their faces

Averted, as if they were watching it take place.

In the casinos, these two lovebirds would lie there
Absorbed in it, staring beyond the green felt

Counters of roulette & baccarat tables, beyond the action,
Beyond the men & women in formal attire.

❧

Then someone told me what the money meant,
What they kept looking at:

They were watching the State wither away.

When I tried to imagine it, all I could see
Was a past

Where the ancient goat paths began reappearing,
Crisscrossing a straighter footpath,

Nothing else there except three pedestals lost in moss,

And a man washing a cart horse with soap & tepid
Water, &, at that moment, placing

A plaster of sticky leaves over the sores on the horse's

Withers, the long muscle in the mare's neck rippling
As he does so, as she goes on grazing without the slightest

Interruption, standing there in the shade of an oak
At the exact spot where the Palace of Justice

Finally turned into the mist it had always resembled.
In the moment before it vanished

Flies still buzzed in lopsided circles in the courtroom

And a witness accidentally inhaled one while testifying,
And then *apologized* to the court, apologized

For inhaling a fly, but no one knew what to say,
The room grew suddenly quiet, & then everything disappeared,

And a crowd strolled out of the matinee into a village
That was waiting for them, strolled casually

Out of history,

And into something else: forgetful, inexact,

A thirst, an arousal, a pairing off with whomever they desired,

Strangers even, trysting against walls,

Or in a field of dandelions, on wagonbeds, the moment
Scripted in the involuntary,

Lovely convulsion of thighs lathered as a horse's back,
Because, as Marx said,

Sex should be no more important than a glass of water.

࿎

I can't imagine it back.

I can't get the miles of dust rubbed away from it,
Or the layers of sheetrock.

The fruitseller's stand on Lomina Street with its closed
Green shutters was what

Reminded me of Big Sur in 1967,

Reminded me of the beach at Lucia with the vacant
Concession stand, the two unemployables

Entwined like salt in a wave inside it, asleep,
Naked in each other's arms.

I can't imagine it enough.

I can't imagine how to get back to it, with something
In your eye, something always in your eye,

And everything becoming a scrap of paper:

The sprawl of the surf there & the cries of the lovers
Just pin-ups or illustrations behind the counter now:

"Gimme a Coke. Gimme a hot dog too, then," someone
Says to him, tattoos from the navy over

His forearms, not liking what he does, not
Imagining doing anything else now

Except this. Just this.

What withered away?

I watch the guy working fast & suddenly it's *me* who's

Wrapping the hot dogs in waxed paper, *me* who
Half turns, grabs the lids & straws for the Cokes,

Adds it up without pausing & hands them the change.

I can't imagine it enough, & even if I could, one day

That, too, would be the wave's sprawl on the empty rocks,
The hunger in the cries of the gulls.

He pulls the shutters down & locks it up.

"Gimme This & Gimme That. You O.K., Mr. Sea?"
He says to the sky, to the gulls,

To the slur of water receding
On the rocks, to the empty sprawl of the wave

Showing its hand at last before it folds.

II

The lovers must have stepped out of their money
A few days after the State stepped out

Of its thousand offices.

At night you could look up, & all the black glass
Of the windows would glint back at you

Once, as if in recognition.

The lovers must have stepped out because I *saw* them

Sitting at one of the tables outside the Moskva & shouting
At each other, shouting so loudly

They did not notice their friends beginning
To gather around them.

I gazed past them at the crowds on Terazije passing by
Amid the smells of exhaust

And grilled meat & the odor the sticky bark of the trees
Gave off in the summer afternoon,

The leaves still & exhausted & not turning or
Falling or doing anything yet

Above it all. I liked them. I liked the way the leaves
Had a right to be there & say nothing about it

Hanging there, motionless, without expression,
Without faces, not looking at all

Like passing generations but exactly as leaves look

When they're still, looking as if
They are refusing to enlist, looking as they always did,

If I glanced up from the book I was reading,
And rubbed my eyes,

And tried to trace her shape I had thought
I'd memorized,

But hadn't.

Her shape like the sun on the roads.

❧

Too bad, with all the evacuations,
All the troop movements & closed offices,

Each black window shining like a contradiction,

"You'd think the Parliament would . . .
You would think out of common *decency,* that . . ."

But the State did not wither away,
It looked just the same, with the rain

Falling between the treeless, bleached yellow
Of cheap housing projects, the rain

Showing them the way home, showing them the Future:

When they get there they find her uncle living
With them, he's eating dinner

When they arrive, he's sucking on a fish bone
When they walk in.

In a few weeks Failure & Limitation
Shows its hand in the cold bud

Of her body refusing to open itself,
Refusing to wake up in the morning,

And the uncle by the end of summer walking naked
Through the apartment, pausing one day

Beside her, leaning over her a little, not to
Seduce her but to show her a few things,

To introduce her to

The real head of state grinning through its veil

Of skin as if there was

This joke, something just between

The two of them.
And later the uncle just grins at her,

Grins & says nothing.

❧

Love's an immigrant, it shows itself in its work.
It works for almost nothing.

When the State withers away it resembles
The poor sections of Wichita or Denver.

They held hands the first day & walked under the trees,
And so they were warned about the trees,

About straying into the parks.

A fuzzy haze of green in someone's yard comes back,
But then it forgets it's there.

The streets are forgetting they are streets
And they cross other streets

And at the intersections those streets
Begin to forget.

Most of the stores are boarded up, most of what
Is left is braced with two-by-fours in X's

Over the doors like spells with no power in them,
The sun like neglect bathing the walls,

Bathing the beams you can see right through to,

It's always the day after the day after here,
And every rebellion's a riot,

The riot goes on though no one's there, the streets
Looking burned still, looking as inexplicable

To them as it did the first day
They saw it,

The *days* are inexplicable,
Their unvarying routine where children not yet

In school peer through the chain link
Of a storm fence above the boulevard & the traffic

To watch for cops,

Where their older brothers with their girlfriends
Sprawl on a car seat ripped out

Of a van & placed here to overlook the city, the river,
Its history an insult in which

They were property.

When it was over, history became a withered arm,
And everyone entered history & no one could find them.

The children keep staring through the chain links

Of the storm fence. The older ones on the car seat
Get high from a glass pipe & watch

The planes on the runway taxi & take off,
They get high again & watch the planes

Glide in & land, & do one last hit before
They stand up & one of them pisses into a small ravine

Of trash. The five-year-old girl keeps peering
Through the storm fence without letting

Her attention stray

Because the price of freedom is eternal vigilance,
Her brother tells her, laughing,

And because the task assigned to her is sacred.
I can't imagine her enough.

I remember standing in broken glass at the foot
Of a stairway, the woman beside me

Frightened & crying, & the way the glass felt
Like a river freezing under my feet.

I remember how expensive it all seemed,

And after we had split up, in the years that followed.
I would feel my body turn

Slowly away from others so that it could live alone,
So that each afternoon it could

Become wholly a body. It swept the floors of the house
Each day until it was a routine,

Until it became the finite, thoughtless beauty
Of habit.

Whenever the body swept, it could forget.

And the habit was neither pleasure nor work but an act
That kept the stars above it

In the night, kept the pattern of the stars
From rattling out of their frames,

Whether you could see them above you or not,
Whether you looked up & noticed them or not,

The body swept the floors & kept the light above it.

This is why

The girl keeps squinting through the storm fence,
This is why the task assigned to her is sacred,

Why her love for her brother
Is unconditional,

And though she suspects that her brother
Will one day turn into mist behind her,

A space on the car seat, that he will
Disappear like the others have,

It hasn't happened yet.

I swept the floors to let the worlds blur
Into one another.

But the lovers, the emigrants?
I never see them anymore.

I don't know where they went.

III

I remember the idiot in the park near Zeleni Venac,
Standing there without a shirt on,

With his fly undone,

The way he'd hold his penis in one hand, & simply howl
And keep howling to anyone passing by

On Lomina Street, because, as Ratko explained it to me,
He believed that he held one end of a leash

In his hand, & that the other end was held by his Master,
And now that it had been snapped in two

He would never find him, this Master he had waited for,
This owner whose whistle he listened for

In the faint blue stillness of the summer daybreak.

In the mornings he would seem calm & play cards
Without understanding them with the others

Who slept in the park & tolerated him, but by
Late afternoon he would begin

To stammer & beg beside the dry fountain, the pine needles
So dry by now they seemed

About to ignite above him, & then, at the certain moment,
He would seem to realize

What had happened, he would become completely still
At that moment, & then . . .

Then the howling would start up again.
It was not the howling of an idea.

It was the flesh being flayed.

My friend Ratko used to drink brandy constantly

In little sips throughout the day & could lie
So beautifully about anything

That the government awarded him, each year, a grant

To write stories, but of course he never wrote them
Except on the air as he walked with friends

Through the city.

Continuing his almost endless commentary,
Asking if the idiot did not admit, without knowing it,

The great truth

About us, that a broken string or snipped-off thread
Is all we remember, & that even this is

Less real than the pulpy flesh he held between his fingers.

History has a withered arm.

And the love of these two adhering to paper, delusional,
Vestigial, the daydream of Capitalism,

The last transaction of the State by which it vanishes,

The flies caking the face of the horse standing there
In its innocence again,

I can't imagine them enough to bring them back.
After a while, when any subject is forbidden,

All thought is deviationist.

And the young schoolteacher in Rijeka is . . . *where* by now?
And the young Muslim poet from Sarajevo is . . . *where* by now?

And the harmless, lazy bellman at the Atina Palace is . . .
Where by now?

And the pipe-smoking translator with his office overlooking
Princip Street & the river,

Who was last heard on the phone shouting to someone
As the beams & window glass let go of themselves

In the laughter that shatters all things is . . . *where* by now?

❧

Those nights when I couldn't sleep in Belgrade,
When I could no longer read,

When there was no point in going out because everything
Was closed, I'd glance at the two of them

On their worthless currency, as if I might catch them
Doing something else, & once,

I turned from their portrait to the empty street
Beneath the window, the thick trees like a stillness

Itself in the night,
And . . . I *saw* them there. This time they were

Fucking in the rain, their clothes strewn beneath them

On the street like flags

After a war, after some final defeat—fucking each other
While standing up, standing still in the rain & the rain falling

In sheets as if there were no tomorrow left
In it, as if their mouths, each wide open & pressed against

The other's mouth, stilling the other's, & reminding me
Of leaves plastered to the back of a horse

Trotting past after a storm, leaves plastered to the side
Of a house by the wind, to what is left of some face . . .

Had taken the breath out of everything. I thought of
The horse passing easily

Under the exhausted-looking mulberry trees, under the leaves
And the haunted scripture—

Some of its characters shaped like blossoms, others
Like a family of crows taking flight, others like farm tools,

Some of them moving in circles like swirls in a current—

All of it written in the cracked, weathered Cyrillic of some
Indecipherable defeat, though once its shapes had been

Perfect for showing one things, clear as a girl's face,

The girl who skipped rope in her communion dress,
                    Dry & white as a petal—

            Jedan. Cesto?, Nema, Zar ne?
                    Chaste & thoughtless as the thing she chanted

And then lost interest in, until I could hear only the endless,
Annoying, unvarying flick of the rope each time

It touched the street.

Acknowledgments

Many thanks to the following magazines and periodicals, where some of the poems in this book have appeared: *American Poetry Review* ("Anastasia and Sandman," "Elegy with a Petty Thief in the Rigging," "The Smell of the Sea," "The Thief in the Painting"); *Field* ("Elegy with a Sprawl of a Wave Inside It"); *New Virginia Review* ("Two Trees"); *Ploughshares* ("Elegy for Whatever Had a Pattern in It"); *Poetry* ("Elegy with a Chimneysweep Falling Inside It"); *Poetry International* ("The Cook Grew Lost in His Village, the Village in the Endless Shuffling of Their Cards"); *Quarterly West* ("Elegy Ending in the Sound of a Skipping Rope"); *Salt Hill Journal* ("In 1967"); *Southern Review* ("Elegy with a Bridle in Its Hand," "Elegy with a Thimbleful of Water in a Cage," "Shiloh"); *Virginia Quarterly Review* ("Elegy for Poe with the Music of a Carnival Inside It"); *Western Humanities Review* ("Elegy with an Angel at Its Gate"). "Anastasia and Sandman" also is in *Best American Poetry 1996*.

Many thanks to these institutions and people who gave time and support to the preparation of the manuscript of these poems: the department of English, Virginia Commonwealth University; New Virginia Review, Inc.; Jan Dougherty; Rose Elliott; Richard Fine; Ann Glenn; Michael Keller; Randy Marshall; Andrew Miller; Josh Poteat; John Venable; Margaret Vopel; and Cheryl Walsh.

LARRY LEVIS

was a native of California and was educated at California State University at Fresno, Syracuse University, and the University of Iowa. He published five collections of poems during his life, the most recent of which was *The Widening Spell of the Leaves* (University of Pittsburgh Press, 1991), as well as a collection of stories, *Black Freckles* (Peregrin Smith, 1992). At the time of his death in May 1996, he was professor of English at Virginia Commonwealth University in Richmond, Virginia, and he had taught previously at the University of Missouri, the University of Utah, the University of Iowa, and in the Warren Wilson Creative Writing Program. His awards include the U.S. Award of the International Poetry Forum, a Lamont Prize, and selection for the National Poetry Series. He received fellowships from the National Endowment for the Arts and the Guggenheim Foundation, and an individual artist's grant from the Virginia Commission for the Arts. In 1989, he was a senior Fulbright fellow in Yugoslavia. His work has appeared in *American Poetry Review*, *Southern Review*, *Field*, and *Iowa Review*, as well as in other magazines.

Library of Congress Cataloging-in-Publication Data

Levis, Larry.
    Elegy / Larry Levis.
        p.   cm — (Pitt poetry series)
    ISBN 0-8229-4043-4 (alk. paper). — ISBN 0-8229-5648-9 (pbk. :
alk. paper)
        I. Title. II. Series.
    PS3562.E922E44 1997
    811'.54 — dc21   97-21097